My Parents Live in Different Houses

Written and Illustrated By Jeff Piper

My Parents Live in Different Houses

My
Parents Live
in
Different Houses

By
Jeffrey S. Piper

My Parents Live in Different Houses
Written and Illustrated by Jeffrey S. Piper
© 2012

ISBN-13: 978-1478233091
ISBN-10: 1478233095

For Kyle, Benjamin, and Grayson for showing me what the love of a parent is all about.

And to all my parents who showed me the world and their love through their different parenting styles.

Hi, my name is Kyle. My parents live in different houses. I live at my mom's house and visit my dad's place a lot. I love both my parents very much.

Because my parents live in different houses, some of the things they do are very different. Sometimes I get confused about whose rules I'm supposed to be following.

At my mothers house I have chores that I must do.
I have to clean my room every Saturday. During
the week I sweep the living room and clean the dishes
after dinner. I enjoy helping out around the house.

At my father's house I don't have to do any chores. Since I do not see my Dad as much as I see my mom, he likes to spend time playing with me, rather than doing chores.

When I stay all night at my Dad's house I can stay up late because it is usually on the weekend and I do not have to get up early the next morning. Sometimes I watch television until I fall asleep on the couch.

My routine is different at my mom's house than at my Dad's house. I usually get up early in the morning when I'm at my Mom's house. That is why I have a bedtime of 8:00pm during the week. I enjoy bedtime because my Mom reads books to me until I fall asleep.

At my mom's house I have a dog. Her name is Sandy.
It is my job to feed her and sometimes we go on walks.
She likes to sleep in my bed at night. I love having a pet.

We have no pets at my Dad's house. It is nice to take a break from the responsibilities of having a pet. It's like having a small vacation.

At my Mom's house she always cooks breakfast, lunch, and dinner. She makes all my favorite meals for me. I love my mom's cooking.

When I'm with my Dad we eat at restaurants most of the time. It's fun to go out to eat.

My Mom's house is big. I have my own room with a comfortable bed. I have lots of friends in the neighborhood where my Mom lives. I spend a lot of my time playing with all of them.

My Dad lives in an apartment building. I do not have as many friends there, but there is an indoor pool to swim in and a swing set that is always fun to play on. Both my mother and my father's houses have things I enjoy doing.

Both my parents enjoy doing different things with me. When I am with my Mom we go on bike rides, hikes, and sometimes she takes me to get ice cream.

Thank You Mom!

My Dad enjoys playing video games with me. We can play for hours. He also likes to take me to the movies. I like to spend time with both my mother and my father so I can do all these things.

Sometimes I get sad because my parents live in different houses. It seems as if I am always traveling between my mom's and Dad's houses. That makes me tired.

Then I think about all the different experiences I have because they live in different houses. I go on bike rides, and get to play video games. I get to go out to eat at restaurants and enjoy home cooked meals. I have learned to take care of a pet, and I can also enjoy the time when I have no responsibility. But most importantly, I know that where ever I go, I am loved.

Use the Space below to list all your favorite things
about your two houses.

My Parents Live in Different Houses is a book designed to help children cope with the living situations that come from a separated or divorced family, an all too common situation in today's society. The goal of the book was to show children that even though it may be very different to go from one house to the other, it can also be fun. This book will be important to young children and parents who are dealing with separation or divorce because it helps children identify the positive aspects of the often difficult transition of traveling between two houses.

My inspiration for this book came from my own childhood. At a very young age, my mother and father divorced and both remarried shortly after. I can remember being confused when my father would come to pick me up to go to his house for the day or weekend. I was entering a new world of rules, traditions, and family members. Routine and structure are important for children; however, separation and divorce, especially during the early stages, often creates imbalance with daily routines. My hopes in writing this book are that children can quickly discover the joys, rather than the sadness, of living in two houses.

Though I feel there is no quick fix for these very real family situations, I do think that this book will help parents and children look at the positive aspects of this reality. The situation will obviously be different for every child, but I encourage you to use this book as a tool for teaching children how to verbally express their thoughts and emotions so that they can relieve anxiety and cope with a complex living arrangement in a healthy way.

Printed in Great Britain
by Amazon